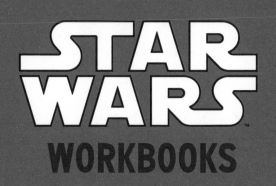

WORKBOOKS

WRITING SKILLS

FOR AGES 7-8

BY THE EDITORS OF BRAIN QUEST

SCHOLASTIC

Scholastic Children's Books
Euston House,
24 Eversholt Street,
London NW1 1DB, UK

A division of Scholastic Ltd
London ~ New York ~ Toronto ~ Sydney ~ Auckland
Mexico City ~ New Delhi ~ Hong Kong

First published in the USA by Workman Publishing in 2014.
This edition published in the UK by Scholastic Ltd in 2015.

© & TM 2015 LUCASFILM LTD.

STAR WARS is a registered trademark of Lucasfilm Ltd.
BRAIN QUEST is a registered trademark of Workman Publishing Co., Inc., and Groupe Play Bac, S.A.

Workbook series design by Raquel Jaramillo
Cover illustration by Mike Sutfin
Interior illustrations by Alitha Martinez

ISBN 978 1407 16282 9

Printed in the UK by Bell and Bain Ltd, Glasgow

4 6 8 10 9 7 5 3

STAR WARS™

WORKBOOKS

This workbook belongs to:

_____

My Favourite Jedi!

Here are six Jedi.

Complete the sentence about one of them.

My favourite Jedi is _____

because _____ .

Draw a picture of your favourite Jedi in action.

Write a sentence about the picture.

_____

_____

_____

Be a Jedi!

Imagine you are training to become a Jedi.
Answer the questions in complete sentences.

What would your Jedi name be?

_____

_____

_____

What colour would your lightsaber be?

_____

What kind of special powers would you have?

_____

_____

_____

_____

Draw a picture of yourself as a Jedi.

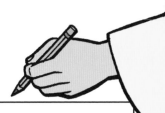

Write a sentence about the picture.

_____

_____

_____

My Favourite Sith!

Here are four Sith.

Complete the sentence about one of them.

My favourite Sith is _____

because _____ .

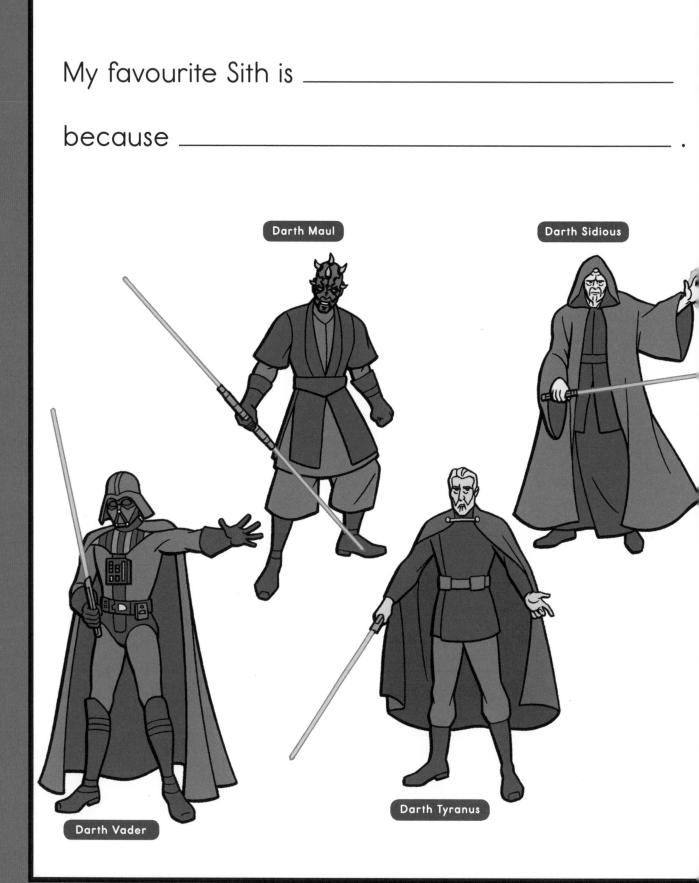

Darth Maul

Darth Sidious

Darth Vader

Darth Tyranus

Draw a picture of your favourite Sith in action.

Write a sentence about the picture.

_____

_____

_____

My Favourite Bounty Hunter!

Here are seven bounty hunters.

Complete the sentence about one of them.

My favourite bounty hunter is _____

because _____ .

Draw a picture of your favourite bounty hunter in action.

Write a sentence about the picture.

_____

_____

_____

The Separatists

Here are five members of the Separatist Alliance.

Complete the sentence about one of them.

My favourite Separatist is _____

because _____ .

Draw a picture of your favourite Separatist in action.

Write a sentence about the picture.

_____

_____

_____

The Galactic Republic

Here are five members of the Galactic Republic.

Complete the sentence about one of them.

My favourite Senator is _____

because _____ .

Chancellor Valorum

Senator Palpatine

Senator Bail Organa

Senator Binks

Senator Padmé

Draw a picture of your favourite Senator in action.

Write a sentence about the picture.

_____

_____

_____

The Rebel Alliance

Here are six Rebels.

Complete the sentence about one of them.

My favourite Rebel is _____

because _____ .

Draw a picture of your favourite Rebel in action.

Write a sentence about the picture.

_____

_____

_____

Clone Commanders

Here are four Clone Commanders.

Complete the sentence about one of them.

My favourite Clone Commander is

_____

because _____ .

Commander Bly

Captain Rex

Commander Cody

Commander Gree

Draw a picture of your favourite Clone Commander in action.

Write a sentence about the picture.

_____

_____

_____

Creatures

Here are three creatures.

Read the sentences about them.

Then use the word **and** to join the two sentences together.

The reek runs. The reek roars.

_____

The rancor is tall. The rancor is strong.

_____

_____

The acklay has sharp claws. It is wild.

_____

_____

reek   rancor   acklay

Imagine a New Creature

Imagine a brand-new creature. Draw a picture here.

What is the name of your creature?

_____

Write a sentence about your new creature.

_____

_____

_____

Species

Write a sentence describing four of the alien species below.

What do they look like?

(You may use the **describing words** from the boxes at the bottom of the page.)

The Twi'lek is blue.

_____

_____

_____

_____

_____

Describing words:

fierce   furry   clumsy

tall   small   blue   big

More Describing Words

Write each of these **describing words** two times.

beautiful _____ _____

great _____ _____

tiny _____ _____

quick _____ _____

clever _____ _____

huge _____ _____

brave _____ _____

wild _____ _____

round _____ _____

cold _____ _____

sharp _____ _____

long _____ _____

Imagine a New Species

Imagine a new type of species.

Draw a picture of your species.

Use some of the **describing words** from the previous pages to write five or more sentences about your species.

_____

_____

_____

_____

_____

_____

_____

_____

_____

_____

Droids!

Look at the droids. Write a sentence about what each droid is doing. (You may use the **action words** from the boxes at the bottom of the page.)

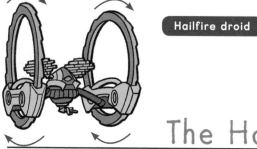
Hailfire droid

The Hailfire droid spins.

battle droid

astromech droid

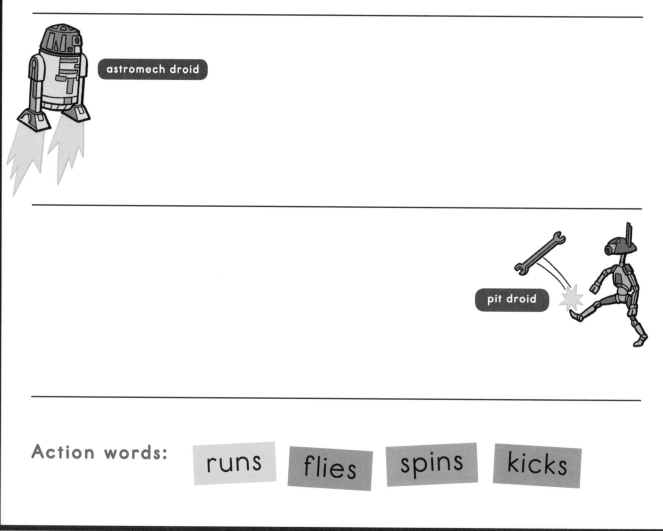
pit droid

Action words: runs   flies   spins   kicks

More Action Words

Write each of these **action words** two times.

speaks

_____   _____

jumps

_____   _____

throws

_____   _____

listens

_____   _____

retries

_____   _____

shakes

_____   _____

fights

_____   _____

reads

_____   _____

learns

_____   _____

spills

_____   _____

dances

_____   _____

drives

_____   _____

writes

_____   _____

Imagine New Droids

Imagine four new types of droids.

Draw a picture of your droids doing something.

Use some of the **action words** from the previous pages to write a sentence about each of your droids.

_____

_____

_____

_____

_____

_____

_____

_____

_____

Gungans

Draw a line from the Gungan to the matching **feeling word**.

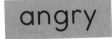
angry

afraid

glad

thoughtful

surprised

More Feeling Words

Write each of these **feeling words** two times.

cheerful _____ _____

happy _____ _____

safe _____ _____

proud _____ _____

angry _____ _____

wonderful _____ _____

confident _____ _____

alarmed _____ _____

shy _____ _____

calm _____ _____

hopeful _____ _____

nervous _____ _____

Write About Geonosis!

Look at this picture of the Geonosian Battle Arena.

Write two sentences that explain what is happening in the picture.
Use **describing**, **action** and **feeling** words.

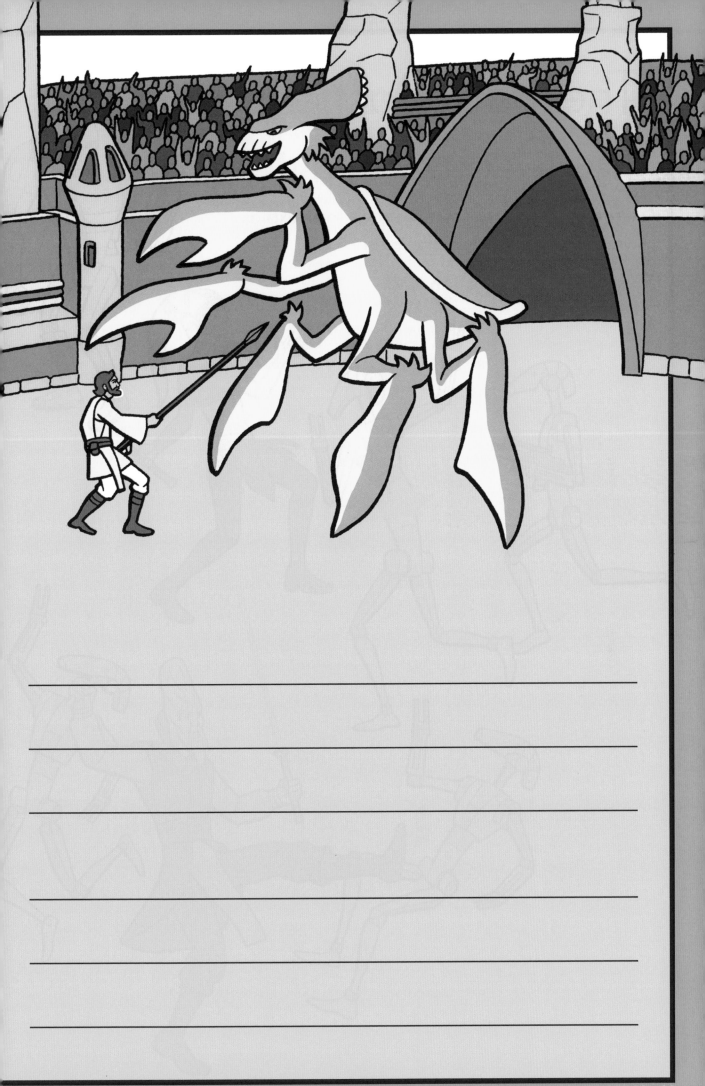

The Jedi Battle the Droid Army

Write three or more sentences that explain what is happening in the picture.

Use **describing**, **action** and **feeling** words.

_____

_____

_____

_____

_____

_____

_____

_____

_____

Jar Jar Binks Falls Down

Write three or more sentences that explain what is happening in the picture.

Use **describing**, **action** and **feeling** words.

Anakin and Shmi Say Goodbye

Write three or more sentences that explain what Anakin and Shmi might be **feeling**.

Luke Fights Darth Vader

Write three or more sentences that explain what Luke might be **feeling** as he battles his father.

A Letter Home

Anakin leaves home to become a Jedi. If you were training to become a Jedi, what letter would you write home? What things would you write about? What feelings would you have? Would you write about some of your adventures?

On the next page, write a letter to someone about your experiences at the Jedi Academy.

Today's date _____

Dear _____ ,

_____

_____

_____

_____

_____

_____

_____

From _____

Tatooine

Homophones are words that sound the same but have different spellings and meanings.

Circle the correct **homophone** to finish each sentence.

Then copy the sentence on the lines below.

Tatooine has two suns   sons .

_____

On Tatooine, Tusken Raiders build tents two   to live in.

_____

_____

They where   wear tan-coloured robes.

_____

_____

Anakin nose knows that he must leave Tatooine to train to become a Jedi.

_____

_____

Becoming a Jedi is the right write thing for Anakin to do.

_____

_____

It will be hard for Anakin to say buy bye to his mother, though.

_____

_____

Jedi Friends

Rewrite the sentences. Use one of the words listed below in the boxes to replace the underlined word in each sentence.

glad   fast

strong   mad

leaps   brave

speaks   shuts

Aayla Secura is <u>happy</u> to see Kit Fisto.

<u>Aayla Secura is glad to see Kit Fisto</u>

Luminara Unduli is <u>quick</u>.

_____

Mace Windu is <u>heroic</u>.

_____

Qui-Gon Jinn <u>jumps</u> in the air.

_____

Yoda <u>talks</u> to Luke.

_____

The Force is <u>powerful</u>.

_____

Anakin looks <u>angry</u>.

_____

Plo Koon <u>closes</u> the door.

_____

Write a Letter to a Jedi

Imagine that you are writing a letter to one of your favourite Jedi.

Tell the Jedi something about yourself.

Ask the Jedi a question about something you would like to know.

_____

_____

_____

_____

_____

_____

_____

_____

_____

A Jedi Riddle Game

Play this game with a friend.

Think about a Jedi, but don't tell your friends.

Write a few sentences to describe this Jedi.

Read your sentences to your friend.

Can your friend guess the name of the Jedi?

_____

_____

_____

_____

_____

_____

_____

Boba Fett

Look at the picture. Read the facts about Boba Fett.

- Boba Fett is a bounty hunter.

- Boba Fett's father was Jango Fett.

- Boba Fett was a boy when Jango Fett was killed.

- Boba Fett uses a jetpack.

- Boba Fett has a blaster.

- Boba Fett wears green battle armour.

Using these facts, write a paragraph to tell us about Boba Fett in an interesting way. Add details to make the story exciting.

_____

_____

_____

_____

_____

_____

_____

_____

Kaminoans

Look at the picture.

Read the facts about Kaminoans.

- Kaminoans are a tall and thin species.

- Kaminoans have large eyes.

- Kaminoans come from the planet Kamino.

- Kaminoans do not express their emotions.

- Kaminoans cloned Jango Fett to create the clone army.

- Lama Su is the prime minister of Kamino.

- Taun We is the name of Lama Su's assistant.

Using these facts, write a paragraph to tell us about Kaminoans in a more interesting way. Add details to make the story more exciting.

_____

_____

_____

_____

_____

_____

_____

Ask a Jedi

Use the **question word** in the box to write a question for the Jedi. Then write what you think the Jedi would answer.

who

Luminara Unduli

what

Plo Koon

where

Aayla Secura

when

Kit Fisto

how

Yoda

Mystery Alien

Imagine a brand-new alien species.

Draw a picture here.

Answer the questions about your new alien species.

1. When was it born?

_____

2. Where does it come from?

_____

_____

3. What does it look and sound like?

_____

_____

4. How does it move?

_____

_____

5. Who is it friends with?

_____

_____

Fill Me In!

This story is about a training school for Jedi on a distant planet.
Read the story and fill in the missing words.

Title: _____

I am training to become a _____ . Today is
(noun)

my _____ day of school. I am here with my best friend
(number)

_____ . Our favourite part of the day is when
(name)

we _____ . We have a _____
(action word)   (adjective)

teacher who can be very strict. Sometimes she makes us

_____ . One time I gave her a _____ .
(verb)   (noun)

Our school is on _____ . There are lots of
(planet name)

_____ here. When we're not training, we spend
(plural noun)

a lot of time _____ and _____ . When I
(verb)   (verb)

get homesick, I _____ to take my mind
(activity)

off it. The _____ is strong with me!
(noun)

Draw a picture to go with your story.

Write a Review!

Have you seen all of the *Star Wars* movies? Write a movie review of your favourite one.

Movie title:

_____

_____

Starring:

_____

_____

What is the movie about?

_____

_____

_____

_____

Draw a picture of your favourite scene.

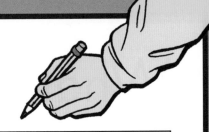

What Happens Next?

Read the beginning of this story.

Last night I had the strangest dream. I dreamt that I was a Jedi. I had the power to hear people's thoughts. Everywhere I went, I could hear what other people were thinking. It was so cool!

What was even cooler, though, was what happened to me after I realized I could hear other people's thoughts. I felt a flutter on my back. I thought someone had bumped into me at first. But when I looked behind me, there was no one there. And that's when I first saw the feathers. I had wings! Not little ones, but big, beautiful wings coming out of my back!

That's when things started to get really crazy...

Write about what happens next. You could always talk through your ideas with a friend.

_____

_____

_____

_____

_____

_____

_____

_____

_____

_____

Finish the Story

Read the beginning of this story.

Write about what happens next.

Then draw a picture.

I am a clone trooper. I am programmed to follow orders.

I was on a mission with the Clone Commander the other day. We were on the planet...

Queen Amidala's Poem

Read this **poem**.

The People's Throne

by Queen Amidala

In this palace full of dreams

I try to lead my people,

To go where I am needed,

To do what must be done.

I cannot watch them suffer

While the politicians argue,

I cannot sit upon a throne

That is too weak to hold us all.

Now write your own **poem**. You could perhaps write in the first person, describe what happens and why, and describe feelings.

_____

_____

_____

_____

_____

_____

_____

_____

_____

_____

Story Time

Write a **story** using any (or all!)
of the made-up characters, creatures
and species you have imagined so far.
Set the **story** on a distant planet.
The **story** already has a beginning!

A long time ago in another galaxy far, far away. . .

_____

_____

_____

_____

_____

_____

_____

_____

_____

Draw a picture of your **story**.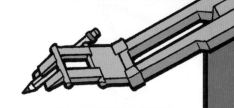

a

Anakin

Trace the letters. Then write them.

a a a a a a

a a a

a a a a a a a

a a a

Trace the words. Then write them.

Anakin

Aayla

acklay

B

Boba Fett

Trace the letters. Then write them.

B B B B B B

B B B

b b b b b b b

b b b

Trace the words. Then write them.

Boba

Bail

Bantha

C

Count Dooku

Trace the letters. Then write them.

C C C C C C

C C C

c c c c c c c

c c c

Trace the words. Then write them.

Count

Coruscant

clone

D

Darth Maul

Trace the letters. Then write them.

$\mathcal{D}$ $\mathcal{D}$ $\mathcal{D}$ $\mathcal{D}$ $\mathcal{D}$ $\mathcal{D}$ $\mathcal{D}$

$\mathcal{D}$ $\mathcal{D}$ $\mathcal{D}$

d d d d d d d

d d d

Trace the words. Then write them.

Darth

Dooku

droid

Emperor

Trace the letters. Then write them.

E E E E E E E

E E E

e e e e e e e

e e e

Trace the words. Then write them.

Emperor

Ewok

energy

F

Fisto

Trace the letters. Then write them.

F F F F F F F F F F F F

F F F

f f f f f f f f f f f f

f f f

Trace the words. Then write them.

Fisto

Force

fan

Grievous

Trace the letters. Then write them.

G G G G G G G

G G G

g g g g g g g

g g g

Trace the words. Then write them.

General

Greedo

galaxy

Han Solo

Trace the letters. Then write them.

𝓗 𝓗 𝓗 𝓗 𝓗 𝓗

𝓗 𝓗 𝓗

h h h h h h h

h h h

Trace the words. Then write them.

Han

Hutt

Human

Imperial Guard

Trace the letters. Then write them.

l l l l l l

l l l

i i i i i i i

i i i

Trace the words. Then write them.

Imperial

inside

interesting

Jar Jar

Trace the letters. Then write them.

Trace the words. Then write them.

Jar Jar

Jedi

jetpack

K

Ki-Adi-Mundi

Trace the letters. Then write them.

$\mathcal{K}$ $\mathcal{K}$ $\mathcal{K}$ $\mathcal{K}$ $\mathcal{K}$ $\mathcal{K}$ $\mathcal{K}$

$\mathcal{K}$ $\mathcal{K}$ $\mathcal{K}$

k k k k k k k

k k k

Trace the words. Then write them.

Ki

Kamino

Kilo

L

Luke

Trace the letters. Then write them.

L L L L L

L L L

l l l l l l l

l l l

Trace the words. Then write them.

Luke

Lando

Lightsaber

M

Mace Windu

Trace the letters. Then write them.

M M M M M

M M M

m m m m m m

m m m

Trace the words. Then write them.

Mace

mynock

monster

Nute Gunray

Trace the letters. Then write them.

$\mathcal{N}$ $\mathcal{N}$ $\mathcal{N}$ $\mathcal{N}$ $\mathcal{N}$ $\mathcal{N}$ $\mathcal{N}$

$\mathcal{N}$ $\mathcal{N}$ $\mathcal{N}$

n n n n n n n

n n n

Trace the words. Then write them.

Nute

Naboo

next

O Obi-Wan

Trace the letters. Then write them.

O O O O O O O O O O O

O O O

O O O O O O O

O O O

Trace the words. Then write them.

Obi-Wan

Organa

orbit

P

Princess Leia

Trace the letters. Then write them.

P P P P P P

P P P

P P P P P P P P

P P P

Trace the words. Then write them.

Princess

Padmé

planet

2 Queen Amidala

Trace the letters. Then write them.

2 2 2 2 2 2

2 2 2

Q Q Q Q Q Q Q

Q Q Q

Trace the words. Then write them.

Queen

Qui-Gon

quarter

R

Rebel Soldier

Trace the letters. Then write them.

R R R R R R R

R R R

n n n n n n n n

n n n

Trace the words. Then write them.

Republic

rancor

reek

Sebulba

Trace the letters. Then write them.

$\mathscr{S}$ $\mathscr{S}$ $\mathscr{S}$ $\mathscr{S}$ $\mathscr{S}$ $\mathscr{S}$

$\mathscr{S}$ $\mathscr{S}$ $\mathscr{S}$

s s s s s s s

s s s

Trace the words. Then write them.

Sebulba

Skywalker

star

T

Tusken Raider

Trace the letters. Then write them.

T T T T T T T

T T T

t t t t t t

t t t

Trace the words. Then write them.

Tusken

Tyranus

tauntaun

U Ugnaught

Trace the letters. Then write them.

U U U U U U U U U

U U U

u u u u u u u u

u u u

Trace the words. Then write them.

Ugnaught

Unduli

under

V

Vader

Trace the letters. Then write them.

$\mathcal{V}$ $\mathcal{V}$ $\mathcal{V}$ $\mathcal{V}$ $\mathcal{V}$ $\mathcal{V}$ $\mathcal{V}$

$\mathcal{V}$ $\mathcal{V}$ $\mathcal{V}$

ν ν ν ν ν ν ν

ν ν ν

Trace the words. Then write them.

Vader

volcano

village

𝓤 Wookiee

Trace the letters. Then write them.

𝓤𝓊 𝓤𝓊 𝓤𝓊 𝓤𝓊 𝓤𝓊

𝓤𝓊 𝓤𝓊 𝓤𝓊

𝓊𝓅 𝓊𝓅 𝓊𝓅 𝓊𝓅 𝓊𝓅 𝓊𝓅 𝓊𝓅

𝓊𝓅 𝓊𝓅 𝓊𝓅

Trace the words. Then write them.

Wookiee

Wedge

wampa

X-wing

Trace the letters. Then write them.

Trace the words. Then write them.

X-wing

X-ray

xylophone

Y

Yoda

Trace the letters. Then write them.

$\mathcal{Y}$ $\mathcal{Y}$ $\mathcal{Y}$ $\mathcal{Y}$ $\mathcal{Y}$ $\mathcal{Y}$

$\mathcal{Y}$ $\mathcal{Y}$ $\mathcal{Y}$

$\mathcal{Y}$ $\mathcal{Y}$ $\mathcal{Y}$ $\mathcal{Y}$ $\mathcal{Y}$ $\mathcal{Y}$

$\mathcal{Y}$ $\mathcal{Y}$ $\mathcal{Y}$

Trace the words. Then write them.

Yoda

youngling

yellow

Zam Wesell

Trace the letters. Then write them.

Trace the words. Then write them.

Zam

Fuckuss

zoom

Answers

Creatures

Here are three creatures.
Read the sentences about them.
Then use the word **and** to join the two sentences together.

The reek runs. The reek roars.
<u>The reek runs and the reek roars.</u>

The rancor is tall. The rancor is strong.
<u>The rancor is tall and the rancor</u>
<u>is strong.</u>

The acklay has sharp claws. It is wild.
<u>The acklay has sharp claws and</u>
<u>it is ferocious.</u>

Gungans

Draw a line from the Gungan to the matching **feeling wo...**

angry

afraid

glad

thoughtfu...

surprised

Tatooine

Homophones are words that sound the same
but have different spellings and meanings.
Circle the correct **homophone** to finish each sentence.
Then copy the sentence on the lines below.

Tatooine has two (suns) sons .

On Tatooine, Tusken Raiders
build tents two (to) ive in.

They where (wear) tan-coloured robes.

Anakin nose (knows) that he must
leave Tatooine to train to become a Jedi.

Becoming a Jedi is the (right) write thing
for Anakin to do.

It will be hard for Anakin to say buy (bye)
to his mother, though.

Jedi Friends

Rewrite the sentences. Use one of the words listed below in
the boxes to replace the underlined word in each sentence.

glad fast
strong mad
leaps brave
speaks shuts

Aayla Secura is <u>happy</u> to see Kit Fisto.
<u>Aayla Secura is glad to see Kit Fisto</u>

Luminara Unduli is <u>quick</u>.
<u>Luminara is fast.</u>

Mace Windu is <u>heroic</u>.
<u>Mace Windu is brave.</u>

Qui-Gon Jinn <u>jumps</u> in the air.
<u>Qui-Gon Jinn leaps in the air.</u>

Yoda <u>talks</u> to Luke.
<u>Yoda speaks to Luke.</u>

The Force is <u>powerful</u>.
<u>The Force is strong.</u>

Anakin looks <u>angry</u>.
<u>Anakin looks mad.</u>

Plo Koon <u>closes</u> the door.
<u>Plo Koon shuts the door.</u>